STAR WARS
REBELS™

BEWARE THE
INQUISITOR!

Written by Lisa Stock

Penguin
Random
House

Written and Edited by Lisa Stock
Editor Anant Sagar
Art Editor Radhika Banerjee
Managing Editors Laura Gilbert,
Chitra Subramanyam
Managing Art Editors Maxine Pedliham,
Neha Ahuja
Art Director Lisa Lanzarini
DTP Designer Umesh Singh Rawat
Pre-Production Producer Marc Staples,
Pre-Production Manager Sunil Sharma
Producer David Appleyard
Reading Consultant Linda B. Gambrell, Ph.D

Publisher Julie Ferris
Publishing Director Simon Beecroft

For Lucasfilm
Executive Editor Jonathan W. Rinzler
Art Director Troy Alders
Story Group Rayne Roberts, Pablo Hidalgo, Leland Chee

First published in the United States in 2015 by DK Publishing
345 Hudson Street, New York, New York 10014

Page design copyright © 2015 Dorling Kindersley Limited
A Penguin Random House Company
10 9 8 7 6 5 4 3 2 1
001–270977–Jan/2015

A CIP catalog record for this book
is available from the Library of Congress.

ISBN: 978-1-4654-2844-8 (Hardback)
ISBN: 978-1-4654-2845-5 (Paperback)

Color Reproduction by Alta Image Ltd, UK
Printed and bound in China by South China Printing Company Ltd.

www.starwars.com
www.dk.com

A WORLD OF IDEAS:
SEE ALL THERE IS TO KNOW

Contents

Who is the Inquisitor?

This scary alien is the Inquisitor. He is from the planet Utapau. The Inquisitor works for the evil Empire that controls the galaxy. He is on the hunt for Jedi who are in hiding.

THE INQUISITOR

Scary tattoos

Double-bladed lightsaber

Round hilt

Arm guard with built-in communicator

Leg guards

FACT FILE

CODE NAME: INQUISITOR

OCCUPATION: JEDI HUNTER

DISTINCTIVE MARK: RED TATTOOS

WEAPON: LIGHTSABER

STRENGTHS

- POWERFUL IN COMBAT
- FEROCIOUS LIGHTSABER FIGHTER
- INTELLIGENT AND CUNNING
- CREATES DEADLY TRAPS

NO LISTED WEAKNESSES

Lothal

The planet of Lothal is very important to the Empire because it is rich in minerals. The Empire does not put up with trouble there. Any rebellion is quickly stamped out.

Rebel Trouble

On Lothal, six rebels have joined together.

They do not like being ruled by the Empire, and they are fighting back!

But beware: The Inquisitor is after the rebels, because he knows that one of them is a Jedi.

ZEB ORRELIOS

WANTED

For injuring Imperial stormtroopers.

EZRA BRIDGER

WANTED

For stealing helmets from the Imperial army and training as a Jedi.

HERA SYNDULLA

WANTED

For beating the Empire's TIE fighters in a space chase.

12

KANAN JARRUS

WANTED

For being a Jedi and
using a lightsaber.
Approach with caution!

SABINE WREN

WANTED

For blowing up Imperial property
with graffiti bombs.

CHOPPER

WANTED

For aggressive attitude
and leaking oil on
Imperial property.

Imperial Army

The Inquisitor is helped by the Empire's army of stormtroopers. These loyal soldiers are trained to protect the Empire at any cost. They spread fear and terror across the galaxy.

STORMTROOPER ARMOR

Standard blaster

Helmet

Shoulder guard

Chest plate

Utility belt

Suit controls

Power cell

Knee guard

Tough shoes

A stormtrooper's armor is fitted with many clever gadgets. These gadgets help the stormtroopers survive their dangerous missions.

Visor

Communicator

Air vent

Breathing filter

Lothal's Imperial Academy

Taskmaster Grint and Commandant Aresko are in charge of training stormtrooper cadets.

The training takes place at Lothal's Imperial Academy. The two agents are cruel and pretty foolish, too!

SERVING THE EMPIRE

Top tips

from the galaxy's toughest officers

Jedi Hunter

Secret Police Agent

⚙ TRAINING TIP

Learn to feel the Force
and never trust the Jedi.

⚙ TRAINING TIP

When tracking rebels,
remember to shoot first
and ask questions later.

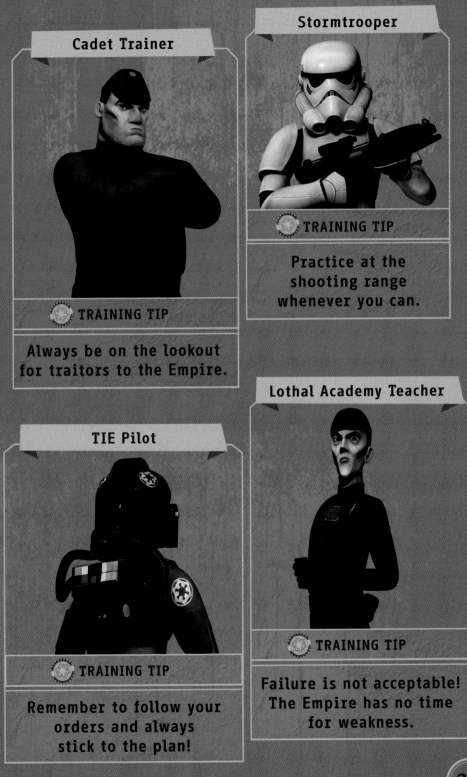

Cadet Trainer

TRAINING TIP

Always be on the lookout for traitors to the Empire.

Stormtrooper

TRAINING TIP

Practice at the shooting range whenever you can.

TIE Pilot

TRAINING TIP

Remember to follow your orders and always stick to the plan!

Lothal Academy Teacher

TRAINING TIP

Failure is not acceptable! The Empire has no time for weakness.

Imperial Navy

The Empire has a fleet
of powerful spaceships.
The most powerful ship
is the Star Destroyer.
It can wipe out a whole
city with one blast.
A Star Destroyer looms
over Lothal.

Secret Agent

Agent Kallus is an officer
of the secret police.
His job is to check that
everyone is following
the Empire's rules.
He discovers that there
are Jedi on Lothal.
This is a job for the Inquisitor!

JEDI ALERT

Agent Kallus knows that he cannot fight the rebels alone. He must call the Inquisitor for help.

Connecting...

SECURE CALL CONNECTED TO THE INQUISITOR

"Excuse the intrusion, Inquisitor. But in the course of my duties, I have encountered a rebel cell. The leader of the cell made good use of a lightsaber."

"Ah, Agent Kallus.
You did well to call.
Now tell me everything
you know about this Jedi."

Receiving...

27

Space Chases

The Empire's TIE fighter spaceships are nimble and very fast.

The Inquisitor flies a
special version named
the TIE Advanced.
This ship is perfect for his
top-secret missions.

TIE ADVANCED

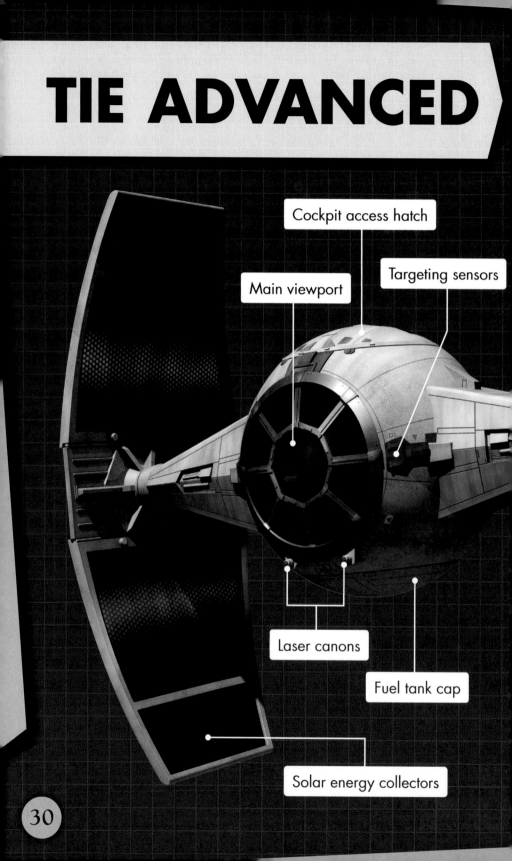

Cockpit access hatch

Main viewport

Targeting sensors

Laser canons

Fuel tank cap

Solar energy collectors

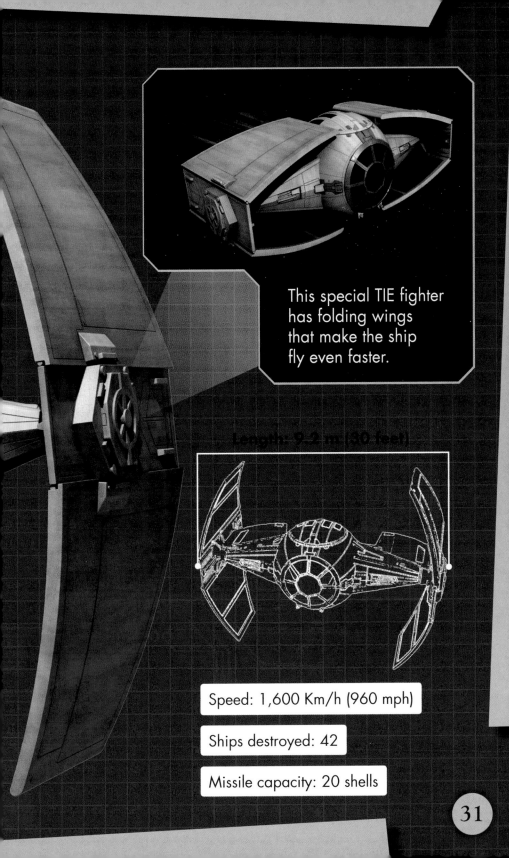

This special TIE fighter has folding wings that make the ship fly even faster.

Length: 9.2 m (30 feet)

Speed: 1,600 Km/h (960 mph)

Ships destroyed: 42

Missile capacity: 20 shells

Capturing Jedi

The Jedi use a special power
called the Force.

The Inquisitor can also
feel the Force.

This means he knows
when a Jedi is near.
He has many tricks and traps
to catch his victims.
There is no place to hide!

PLANNING AN ESCAPE

Ezra's step-by-step guide

1

If an Imperial officer catches you, don't panic!
Make sure you don't let him see that you are afraid.

2

Find a disguise and hide in the air vents.
Stormtrooper helmets have radios. Be sneaky and listen in.

3

Your friends are sure to come to your rescue. Run to your ship as fast as you can, but watch out for stormtroopers.

4

Need a distraction? A big explosion is perfect to keep the Empire off your back while you make your exit.

Great Escape

The Inquisitor lures the
rebels into a trap!
He thinks it will be easy
to defeat them.
But the Jedi rebel named
Kanan is very brave.
He fights with the Inquisitor
until all the rebels
manage to escape.

INQUISITOR'S
MISSION REPORT

MISSION TARGET
Capture rebels on Lothal

MISSION RESULT

FAILURE

Reason for failure:

- Rebels are smarter than expected

- Stormtroopers were beaten

- Traps did not work as planned

- Rebel ship could not be tracked

ANOTHER PLAN IS NEEDED...

Inquisitor's Anger

The rebels were able to
escape this time.
However, they are
not entirely safe.
The Inquisitor is
very angry that he
has failed his mission.
He will not give up
until he has captured
every last Jedi.
Watch out, rebels!

Quiz

1. Which planet is the Inquisitor from?

2. Who is the Inquisitor trying to catch?

3. Which planet is important to the Empire?

4. What are Imperial soldiers called?

5. What is Grint and Aresko's job?

6. What color is the Inquisitor's lightsaber?

7. Which is the most powerful ship in the Imperial navy?

8. Who works for the secret police?

9. What is the name of the Inquisitor's spaceship?

10. Which special power can the Inquisitor feel?

Answers on
page 45

Glossary

Empire
A group of worlds ruled by an Emperor.

Fleet
A group of spacecraft.

Jedi
Beings who use the Force to help others
in the galaxy.

Lightsaber
Weapon used by Jedi and others who can
feel the Force.

Lures
Tempts a person to do something.

Minerals
Something valuable that is
found in the earth.

Rebellion
A group of people not
following the rules.

Index

Answers to the quiz on pages 42 and 43:
1. Utapau 2. The Jedi 3. Lothal 4. Stormtroopers
5. Training stormtrooper cadets 6. Red 7. Star Destroyer
8. Agent Kallus 9. TIE Advanced 10. The Force

Guide for Parents

DK Readers is a four-level interactive reading adventure series for children, developing the habit of reading widely for both pleasure and information. These books have an exciting main narrative interspersed with a range of reading genres to suit your child's reading ability, as required by the Common Core State Standards. Each book is designed to develop your child's reading skills, fluency, grammar awareness, and comprehension in order to build confidence and engagement when reading.

Ready for a *Beginning to Read* book
YOUR CHILD SHOULD

- be able to read many words without needing to stop and break them down into sound parts.
- read smoothly, in phrases and with expression. By this level, your child will be beginning to read silently.
- self-correct when some word or sentence doesn't sound right.

A Valuable and Shared Reading Experience

For some children, text reading, particularly non-fiction, requires much effort, but adult participation can make this both fun and easier. So here are a few tips on how to use this book with your child.

TIP 1 Check out the contents together before your child begins:

- invite your child to check the blurb, contents page, and layout of the book and comment on it.
- ask your child to make predictions about the story.
- talk about the information your child might want to find out.

TIP 2 Encourage fluent and flexible reading:

- support your child to read in fluent, expressive phrases, making full use of punctuation and thinking about the meaning.

- help your child learn to read with expression by choosing a sentence to read aloud and demonstrating how to do this.

TIP 3 Indicators that your child is reading for meaning:

- your child will be responding to the text if he/she is self-correcting and varying his/her voice.
- your child will want to talk about what he/she is reading or is eager to turn the page to find out what will happen next.

TIP 4 Chat at the end of each chapter:

- encourage your child to recall specific details after each chapter.
- let your child pick out interesting words and discuss what they mean.
- talk about what each of you found most interesting or most important.
- ask questions about the text. These help to develop comprehension skills and awareness of the language used.

A FEW ADDITIONAL TIPS

- Read to your child regularly to demonstrate fluency, phrasing, and expression; to find out or check information; and for sharing enjoyment.
- Encourage your child to reread favorite texts to increase reading confidence and fluency.
- Check that your child is reading a range of different types of material, such as poems, jokes, and following instructions.

Series consultant, **Dr. Linda Gambrell**, Distinguished Professor of Education at Clemson University, has served as President of the National Reading Conference, the College Reading Association, and the International Reading Association. She is also reading consultant for the **DK Adventures**.

Have you read these other great books from DK?

BEGINNING TO READ ALONE ②

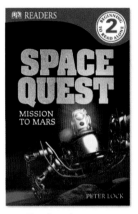

Meet a band of rebels, brave enough to take on the Empire!

Join C-3PO on his exciting adventures across the galaxy.

Embark on a mission to explore the solar system. First stop—Mars.

READING ALONE ③

Learn all about Yoda's battles and how he uses the Force.

Can Luke Skywalker help the rebels defeat the evil Empire?

Meet the sharks who live on the reef or come passing through.